DOG
FACT
FRENZY!

.... **by Nikki Potts** ....

CAPSTONE PRESS
a capstone imprint

Published by Capstone Press, an imprint of Capstone
1710 Roe Crest Drive, North Mankato, Minnesota 56003
capstonepub.com

Dog Fact Frenzy! was originally published as *Totally Amazing Facts About Dogs*, copyright 2019 by Capstone Press.

Library of Congress Cataloging-in-Publication Data is available
on the Library of Congress website.

ISBN: 9798875233609 (hardcover)
ISBN: 9798875233555 (paperback)
ISBN: 9798875233562 (ebook PDF)

Summary: Dog lovers won't be able to put down this collection of browsable facts delivered up with awesome canine photos!

Editorial Credits
Editors: Kristen Mohn and Alison Deering; Designer: Jaime Willems;
Media Researcher: Svetlana Zhurkin; Production Specialist: Whitney Schaefer

Getty Images: Aleksandr Zotov, 21, alkir, 10, CalypsoArt, 12, cynoclub, 18, 31, damedeeso, 52, GlobalP, 9, I love Photo and Apple, 58, iridi, 37; Newscom: Heritage Images/Fine Art Images, 20; Shutterstock: Alexander Ermolaev, 47, 62 (top), Alexander Sorokopud, 49, Andrea Izzotti, 56 (top), Annette Shaff, 25, Anurak Pongpatimet, 36, Asitha P.K0, 15, CkyBe (speech bubbles), cover and throughout, cpaulfell, 19, Creativa Images, 7, cynoclub, 30, David Dirga, 28, Dora Zett, cover (dogs), Dreamer Light (background), cover, back cover, emmanuellegrimaud, 53 (dog), Eric Isselee, 5 (bottom), 27, 34, 64, Erickson Stock, 48, Franco Cesar Buttafuoco, 17, Gajus, 44, Giampaolo Cianella, 8, gn8 (rays and lines), cover and throughout, GoodFocused, 4 (middle), 54, Guppic the duck, cover (sunglasses, tie, party hats), Javier Brosch, 41, Jim Cumming, 6, K9 and photography, 42, kathrineva20, 14, 38, Lelusy, 35, lightman_pic, 23, Ljupco Smokovski, 45, Master1305, 13, Michar Peppenster, 46, MirasWonderland, 4 (left), MR.Yanukit, 60, Natalia Pogodina, 61, New Africa, 55, Olena Kurashova, 39, olgagorovenko, 40, 56, Pixel-Shot, 26, 33, Reddogs, 50, Rob kemp, 59, Rosa Jay, 1 (bottom), 11, seeshooteatrepeat, 53 (rosette), smrm1977, 1 (top), 5 (top), 32, Svetography, 24, Tamim 99Graphics (dog silhouettes), 3 and throughout, Tatiana Gladskikh, 29, The Adaptive, 51, Thiago Diaz, 57, TrapezaStudio, 16, v_kulieva (gradient background), back cover and throughout, Vetlife, 22, vyasphoto, 63, Wasitt Hemwarapornchai, 43, Wisiel, back cover, 4 (right), Yulia YasPe, 62 (bottom)

TABLE OF CONTENTS

A PUP-TASTIC COLLECTION OF CANINE FACTS

Pooch, pup, hound, or mutt—"man's best friend" goes by many names. But how much do you know about your four-legged pal? If you want to know ABSOLUTELY EVERYTHING there is to know about dogs . . . you might have to go back about 15,000 years. But if you want to learn some really cool canine stuff, you came to the right place. From sensational sniffers to the mysteries of "Frito feet," you're about to discover a frenzy of dog facts!

GET READY FOR SOME
BOWWOW KNOW-HOW!

HOUND HISTORY AND FAMOUS FIDOS

Dogs are descended from gray wolves.

Dogs have been domesticated
for at least 15,000 years.

WOW!

THEY WERE THE FIRST ANIMALS
TO BE DOMESTICATED BY HUMANS.

Some ways people first used dogs
were for hunting and protection.

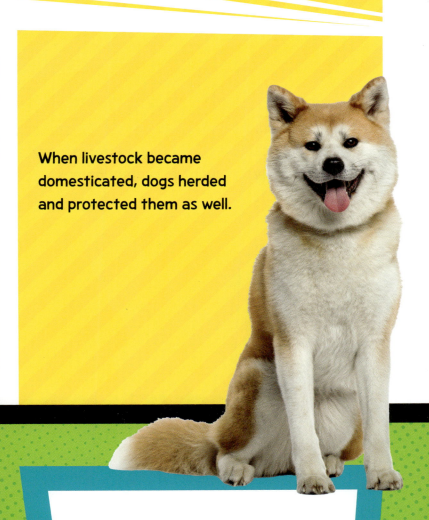

When livestock became domesticated, dogs herded and protected them as well.

Greyhounds, Basenjis, and a type of husky called Akita Inu are among the oldest dog breeds.

The Aztecs worshipped a hairless dog breed called Xoloitzcuintli (show-lo-eets-KWEENT-lee). These dogs were thought to protect homes from evil spirits.

Basenjis were given as gifts to Egyptian pharaohs.

WOW!

BASENJIS DON'T BARK.
THEY YODEL!

Dogs were once banned as pets in Iceland. One reason was because they were considered unclean!

Today there are about 360 dog breeds.

A "designer dog" is one that is bred from more than one dog breed. (For instance, a chiweenie is a cross between a Chihuahua and a dachshund.)

An Australian cattle dog named Bluey lived to be 29 years and 5 months old. He is one of the oldest dogs on record.

WOW!

A DOG'S AVERAGE LIFE SPAN IS 10 TO 13 YEARS.

George Washington loved dogs. He had a French hound named Vulcan and a dalmatian named Madam Moose.

It's said that the Brussels griffon breed was the inspiration for Ewok characters in the Star Wars movies.

Fang from the Harry Potter movies was a Neapolitan mastiff. These dogs can weigh more than 150 pounds (68 kilograms)!

Chihuahuas are the tiniest dogs. One named Miracle Milly weighed just 1 pound (0.5 kg).

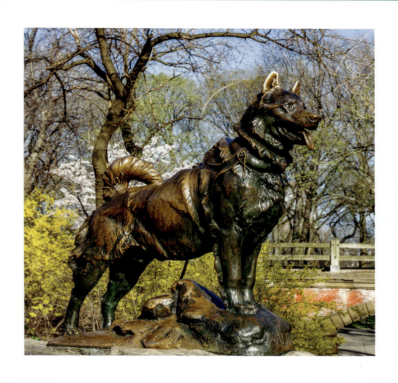

Balto was an Alaskan husky who led a team of sled dogs across Alaska to deliver medicine to sick people in 1925.

A stray dog named Laika from the former Soviet Union became the first "space dog" when she orbited Earth in a spacecraft.

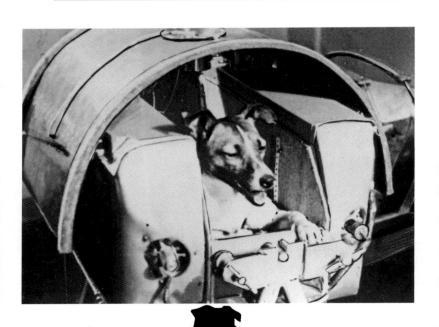

The cartoon dog Scooby-Doo is modeled after a Great Dane.

WOW!

WHEN THEY STAND ON THEIR HIND LEGS, GREAT DANES ARE TALLER THAN MOST HUMANS!

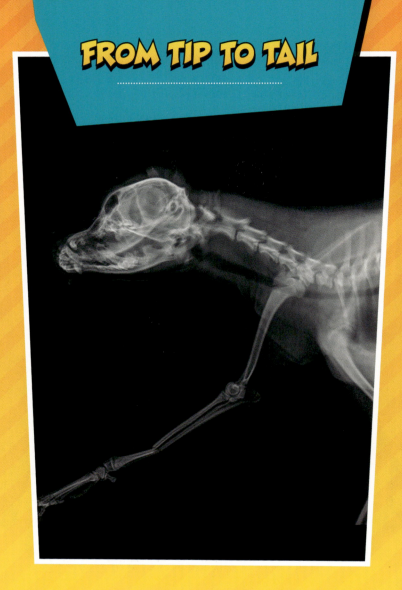

Dogs have about 320 bones.

The wetness of a dog's nose is actually a thin layer of mucus. It helps the dog smell!

Dogs have around 1,700 taste buds. (Humans have about 9,000.)

Most dogs have pink tongues, but chow chow and shar-pei tongues are black.

A dog's normal body temperature is 101 to 102.5 degrees Fahrenheit (38.3–39.2 degrees Celsius).

A small dog's heart beats between 100 and 140 times per minute.

Do your dog's paws smell like corn chips or popcorn? That smell is known as "Frito feet" and is caused by bacteria.

Dogs have some sweat glands in their paws, but panting is their main way of cooling off.

A special membrane in a dog's eyes helps it see at night. It's called the tapetum lucidum.

It is a myth that dogs only see in black and white. They see some color but not as vividly as humans.

WOW!

PUPPIES CAN'T SEE OR HEAR WHEN THEY ARE FIRST BORN.

Puppies have 28 teeth. Adult dogs have 42.

Norwegian lundehunds have
six toes on each foot!

WOW!

NEWFOUNDLANDS HAVE WEBBED FEET TO HELP THEM SWIM. THEY ARE ALSO KNOWN AS "NEWFIES."

Dogs can hear sounds of 35,000 vibrations per second. (Humans can only hear 20,000 vibrations per second.)

Dogs have at least 18 muscles in each ear.

Dogs can shut off their inner ear
to block distracting sounds.

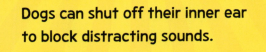

Long ears help some dog breeds gather smells as their ears drag on the ground!

Basset hounds have some of the longest ears of any breed. Some measure 10 inches (25.4 centimeters) long!

Dogs perk up their ears and tilt their heads to determine what a sound is.

DOG JOBS AND SUPER SKILLS

The average dog thinks like a 2-year-old child.

Dogs can learn up to 250 words.

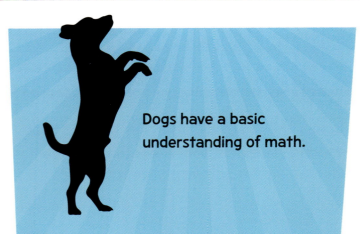

Dogs have a basic understanding of math.

Border collies are one of the smartest dog breeds.

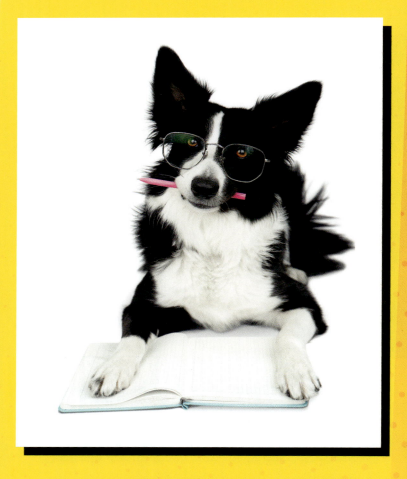

A border collie named Chaser was thought to be the world's smartest dog. She recognized the names of more than 1,000 objects!

Poodles, German shepherds, and golden retrievers are also among the most intelligent dog breeds.

A dog can smell at least 1,000 times better than a human. (It has 200 to 300 scent receptors in its nose.)

Depending on conditions, a dog may be able to smell a person coming from about 10 miles (16 kilometers) away.

WOW!

SOME DOGS ARE ABLE TO SMELL
AND IDENTIFY CANCER IN HUMANS.

The German shepherd is the top police and military dog breed.

Orient, a German shepherd guide dog, successfully led his blind owner through the Appalachian Trail. The trek took eight months.

Service dogs pee and poop on command.

Dogs can be trained to help people who are having seizures. They lie down next to their owners to prevent injury.

A service dog named Kirsch received an honorary degree from Johns Hopkins University. (He attended every class with his owner, Carlos.)

Greyhounds are the fastest dog breed. They can run up to 45 miles (72.4 km) per hour.

Beagles and Siberian huskies are considered the noisiest breeds!

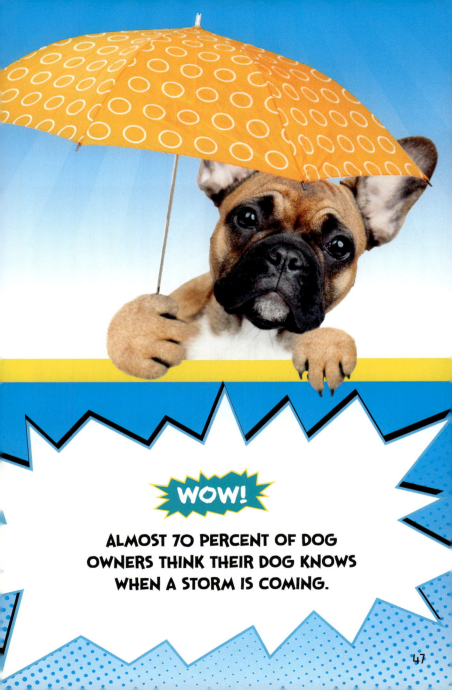

WOW!

ALMOST 70 PERCENT OF DOG
OWNERS THINK THEIR DOG KNOWS
WHEN A STORM IS COMING.

A dog can sense a person's anxiety.

PETTING A DOG CAN LOWER
YOUR BLOOD PRESSURE.

A dog's brain releases the "happy chemical" oxytocin when it spends time with some humans and other dogs.

It is a myth that dogs feel guilt.

Your dog is likely feeling fear instead.

But dogs *can* feel jealous!

CANINE CURIOSITIES

The United States has more dogs than any other country.

There are nearly 90 million pet dogs in the U.S.

A Great Pyrenees named Duke won the mayoral election three times running in Cormorant, Minnesota.

Max and Charlie are the most popular male dog names.

For female dogs, Luna and Bella are the most popular names.

The Labrador retriever has been a top 10 most popular breed more times than any other breed.

A dog's nose print is as unique
as a human's fingerprint.

AAH-CHOO!

Like humans, dogs can
have seasonal allergies.

Dogs can be right-pawed or left-pawed!

One study says that some dogs align themselves with Earth's magnetic field while they poop.

Dog pee can corrode metal.

WOW!

A DOG KICKS WITH ITS BACK FEET AFTER GOING TO THE BATHROOM TO MARK ITS TERRITORY.

More than 40 percent of dogs sleep in bed with their owners.

It is a natural instinct for dogs to spin before lying down.

Dogs naturally curl up when they sleep. This position protects their vital organs and keeps them warm.

Puppies can sleep as much as 20 hours a day!

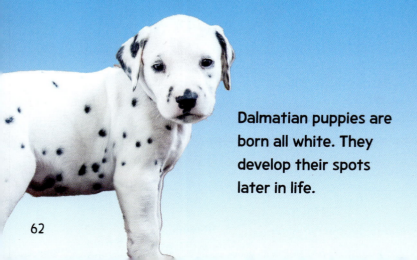

Dalmatian puppies are born all white. They develop their spots later in life.

The most puppies ever born in one litter was 24!

OTHER BOOKS IN THIS SERIES